YAKALOU MEDIA

GET CLARITY ABOUT YOUR PERSONAL FINANCE

100 Questions To Ask Yourself To Understand And Manage Your Personal Finance

Contents

Disclaimer

This book is designed to provide information only. This information is provided and sold with the knowledge that the publisher and author do not offer any legal or other professional advice. In the case of a need for any such expertise, consult with the appropriate professional.

This book does not contain all the information available on the subject. This book has not been created to be specific to any individual's or organization's situation or needs. Every effort has been made to make this book as accurate as possible. However, there may be typographical and/or content errors. Therefore, this book should serve only as a general guide, not as the ultimate source of subject information.

This book contains information that might be dated and is intended only to educate and entertain. Regarding any loss or damage allegedly suffered or alleged to have occurred as a result of the information in this book, either directly or indirectly, the author and publisher shall have no liability or responsibility to any person or entity.

I

BEFORE EVERYTHING

Introduction

Why Understanding Personal Finance is Crucial

Have you ever found yourself pondering at the end of the month, wondering where all your money went? Or perhaps, sitting across the table during a family dinner, you've thought about how to secure your family's future financially. These thoughts are not just passing whims; they're crucial reflections of our need to understand personal finance. It's a subject that touches every aspect of our lives, yet, ironically, it's often the one we're least prepared to handle. So why is getting to grips with personal finance so essential?

Let's start with the basics. Do you know exactly how much you earn and spend each month? The answer might seem straightforward, but for many, it's a puzzle wrapped in layers of bank statements and online transactions. This book begins by unraveling this mystery. We'll dive into simple yet profound questions that shine a light on your income, expenses, and those sneaky little costs that slip through the cracks.

But understanding personal finance isn't just about tracking numbers. It's about setting goals. What are your financial dreams? A house? A comfortable retirement? Maybe even a well-deserved vacation? These aren't just lofty dreams; they're achievable milestones, but only if we plan for them. This book guides you through crafting achievable financial goals tailored to your unique life situation.

Debt, a word that often brings a shiver down our spines, is another critical piece of the puzzle. How do you manage it, reduce it, and eventually live a debt-free life? We'll explore this with practical, straightforward strategies that demystify the complex world of loans, interest rates, and credit scores.

And then, there's the future. How do we ensure that the life we're building today can sustain us tomorrow? We'll delve into the essentials of saving and investing, breaking them down into simple, actionable steps. Whether you're a seasoned saver or a complete novice, this book has nuggets of wisdom for everyone.

Lastly, we'll tackle the often-overlooked yet vital aspects of insurance and taxes. Understanding these can not only save you money but also prevent unforeseen financial disasters.

This book, "Get Clarity About Your Personal Finance," isn't just a collection of financial advice. It's a journey towards financial empowerment. A journey that begins with a question, "Are you ready to take control of your financial future?" Let's embark on this journey together, one question at a time.

How This Book Can Help You

Have you ever felt like your finances are controlling you instead of the other way around? Do you often find yourself puzzled about how to manage your money better? This is where "Get Clarity About Your Personal Finance" steps in. It's more than just a guide; it's your personal finance coach, here to transform your relationship with money.

Think about it: When was the last time you felt truly confident about a financial decision you made? This book aims to make that confidence a regular part of your life. By asking the right questions, we help you uncover the answers that are already within you. These aren't just generic questions, but tailored prompts that guide you through understanding your unique financial situation.

We start by laying a solid foundation. How much do you really know about your finances? This isn't about complex spreadsheets or financial jargon. We're talking about simple, clear insights into how much you earn, spend, and save. This book takes you by the hand and helps you track your financial journey, making sense of each dollar and cent.

But knowledge alone isn't power; it's applying that knowledge that truly empowers. That's why each chapter of this book is designed to not just provide information but to spur you into action. Whether it's setting up a budget, planning for retirement, or tackling debt, we provide practical steps that you can start implementing right away.

Moreover, this book understands that personal finance is just that—personal. Your financial goals and challenges are unique to you. That's why we focus on helping you create a personalized financial plan. This isn't about what works for everyone else; it's about what works for you.

And let's face it, finance can sometimes be a dry topic. But we believe it doesn't have to be. Our approach is to make learning about finance as engaging and relatable as possible. We use everyday language, real-life examples, and a touch of humor to keep you interested and motivated.

In essence, "Get Clarity About Your Personal Finance" is more than a book; it's a tool for life. It's designed to grow with you, offering advice and guidance no matter where you are in your financial journey. Whether you're just starting out, looking to make more informed decisions, or planning for the future, this book is here to help.

So, are you ready to take control of your finances, make informed decisions, and confidently plan for your future? Let's turn the page and start this transformative journey together.

The 5 Rules To Get The Most Out Of This Book

As you embark on this journey to financial clarity and confidence, it's essential to approach this book with the right mindset. "Get Clarity About Your Personal Finance" is more than just a read; it's a practical guide, and to get the most out of it, there are five golden rules you should follow. Additionally, there's a crucial word of warning that we must address.

Rule 1: Be Honest with Yourself

The first rule is simple yet profound: Be honest with yourself. This book will ask you to take a hard look at your finances. Are you ready to face the reality of where you stand financially? The effectiveness of this book hinges on your willingness to be transparent about your income, debts, spending habits, and financial goals. Remember, you're not doing this for anyone else but yourself.

Rule 2: Commit to Taking Action

Next, commit to taking action. It's one thing to read and understand; it's another to put what you've learned into practice. Will you take the steps outlined in each chapter? Whether it's creating a budget, adjusting your spending, or setting up a savings plan, your progress depends on the actions you take after turning each page.

Rule 3: Keep an Open Mind

Keeping an open mind is crucial. Personal finance can be filled with preconceived notions and overwhelming advice. Are you open to new ideas and strategies that may differ from what you've always believed about money management? This book might challenge some of your existing beliefs, but being open to new perspectives is key to growth.

Rule 4: Be Consistent

Consistency is your ally. Can you dedicate time regularly to read, reflect, and implement the suggestions in this book? Consistency doesn't mean you have to overhaul your financial life overnight. Small, consistent actions can lead to significant, lasting change.

Rule 5: Reflect and Revise

Finally, remember to reflect and revise. As you progress through this book, your understanding of your finances will evolve. Are you willing to revisit and adjust your financial plan as you gain more clarity? This book is not a one-time read; it's a guide that you can come back to, refining your approach as your financial situation and goals change.

A Word of Warning

Now, for a word of warning: This book is not a magical solution. It requires effort and dedication from you. It's also important to recognize that everyone's financial journey is different. What works for one person may not work for another. So, while this book provides guidance and best practices, always consider your unique circumstances.

Financial freedom and clarity are within your reach, but they don't come without effort and commitment. By following these five rules and heeding this warning, you're setting yourself up for a rewarding journey. Let's dive in and transform how you view and manage your finances, one page at a time.

Your Journey, Your Way

Welcome to a unique chapter in your journey with "Get Clarity About Your Personal Finance". Here's something you might find surprising: You don't need to read this book from cover to cover, page after page, in a linear fashion. That's right, this isn't your traditional finance book. It's more like a personal finance toolkit, designed to be flexible and adaptable to your individual needs and pace.

Why this approach, you might ask? Because personal finance is not a one-size-fits-all matter,. It's deeply personal, and everyone's financial journey is unique. Some of you might be starting with a blank slate, eager to learn the basics, while others might be halfway through, looking to fine-tune their strategies. That's the beauty of this book—it's crafted to cater to everyone, regardless of where you are on your financial path.

Picture this: It's a quiet Sunday afternoon. You're sitting with a cup of tea, pondering over your financial goals. You don't want to wade through chapters of budgeting advice if your immediate concern is investing. Why not flip directly to the section on investments? The chapters and questions are structured to guide you straight to the information you need, right when you need it.

Each section of this book is a standalone module, focusing on different aspects of personal finance. From budgeting to saving, from investments to taxes, each chapter is an independent resource. They're interconnected yet distinct, allowing you to jump between topics as your interests or needs change. This format is especially useful when a specific financial question arises. You can directly consult the relevant section, find your answer, and apply it to your life without having to sift through unrelated information.

Moreover, we understand that your financial situation can change over time. What seems irrelevant today might become crucial tomorrow. That's why this book is designed for you to revisit. Maybe today you're focusing on paying off debt. A year from now, you might be more interested in retirement planning. This book grows with you, offering valuable insights at each stage of your financial journey.

Let's address a common concern: the overwhelming nature of financial planning. The sheer amount of information available makes it simple to feel overwhelmed. By allowing you to target specific topics or questions, we aim to make your learning process more manageable and less daunting. You can take it one question at a time, at your own pace, without the pressure of following a sequential path.

Essentially, "Get Clarity About Your Personal Finance" is not just a book; it's a lifelong companion on your journey to financial literacy and independence. It's here to provide answers when you have questions, guidance when you're uncertain, and reassurance when you need it. By using this book as a resource to consult as needed, you empower yourself to take control of your financial future in a way that makes sense for you.

So, feel free to jump around, explore the sections that resonate with you at this moment, and know that this book is here to support you, wherever you are on your financial journey. Remember, this is your journey, and you get to navigate it in a way that best suits you.

II

The 100 Questions To Ask Yourself To Understand And Manage Your Personal Finance

Chapter 1: Understanding Your Current Financial Status

Let's start with the story of Emily, a graphic designer in her mid-thirties. Every month, Emily experiences the same cycle: she receives her paycheck, pays her bills, and before she knows it, she's anxiously waiting for the next payday. She wonders where her money goes and why saving seems like a distant dream. Does this sound familiar to you? Many of us, like Emily, face the challenge of understanding our financial status. This chapter is about breaking that cycle and gaining a clear picture of where you stand financially.

Assessing Your Income

Firstly, let's look at income. It's not just about how much you earn, but how you earn it. Is your income consistent, or does it fluctuate? For Emily, her freelance projects mean her income varies month-to-month. This can be both an opportunity and a challenge. Understanding your income pattern is the first step in gaining financial control.

Identifying Your Regular Expenses

Next, we dive into expenses. It's easy to underestimate regular expenses, especially the small ones that add up. Emily started tracking her daily coffee purchases and was surprised to see how much they totaled by month-end. Regular expenses aren't just bills; they're those little things we often overlook.

Understanding Your Savings

Now, let's talk about savings. For many, savings are what's left after spending. But what if we reversed this mindset? Think of savings as a bill that you pay yourself. It's a mindset shift that Emily adopted, and it transformed the way she managed her finances.

Evaluating Your Debts

Finally, debts. They can be overwhelming, but understanding them is crucial. What kind of debts do you have? Are they high-interest debts like credit card balances or long-term debts like a mortgage? Emily realized that paying off her high-interest debts first would save her money in the long run.

So, where do you start to understand your financial status? Here are 10 straightforward questions and one practical exercise to guide you:

1. What is your total monthly income after taxes?
2. List all your regular monthly expenses (rent, utilities, subscriptions).
3. How much do you spend on groceries each month?

4. What are your monthly transportation costs?
5. Do you have any recurring expenses that you might have overlooked (like that daily coffee)?
6. How much do you currently save each month?
7. What percentage of your income goes into savings?
8. List all your debts (credit card, loans, mortgage).
9. What are the interest rates on your debts?
10. Which debts can be paid off quicker to reduce interest?

Understanding your financial status is like laying the foundation of a house. It might not be the most glamorous part, but it's essential for building a stable and secure financial future. Just like Emily, by answering these questions and completing the exercise, you're taking the first critical steps towards financial clarity and empowerment.

Exercise #1

Practical Exercise:

For one month, track every penny you spend. Use a simple spreadsheet or a budgeting app. This will give you a clear picture of where your money is going and highlight areas where you can cut back.

Chapter 2: Setting Financial Goals

Meet Alex, a high school teacher with dreams of traveling the world, owning a home, and ensuring a comfortable retirement. Like many of us, Alex has a variety of goals but struggles to prioritize and plan for them. His story highlights a common dilemma: how do we set and achieve our financial goals?

Short-Term vs. Long-Term Goals

Financial goals vary greatly in their time frame and nature. Alex's dream of a vacation in Europe is a short-term goal, something he wants to achieve within a year. On the other hand, his retirement plan is a long-term goal, spanning several decades. Understanding the difference between these two is crucial. Short-term goals often require more immediate, aggressive savings, while long-term goals can be planned with a more gradual approach.

Prioritizing Your Financial Objectives

Prioritization is key. Not all financial goals carry the same weight. For Alex, buying a home is more important than his travel plans. This meant adjusting his budget to save more for the down payment, even if it meant postponing his vacation. It's about making choices that align with your most crucial objectives.

Creating Achievable Financial Targets

Setting achievable targets is about being realistic. Alex calculated what percentage of his income he could reasonably save each month without compromising his current quality of life. It's a balance between aspirational and practical, ensuring that your goals motivate you rather than frustrate you.

As you embark on your journey to set financial goals, here are 10 questions and a practical exercise to guide you:

1. What are your top three short-term financial goals?
2. What are your top three long-term financial goals?
3. How much money do you need to achieve each of these goals?
4. By when do you want to achieve each of your short-term goals?
5. When do you want to achieve each of your long-term goals?
6. What percentage of your monthly income can you allocate towards these goals?
7. How can you adjust your current spending to allocate more towards your goals?
8. Are there any additional sources of income you can tap into?
9. What sacrifices are you willing to make to achieve these goals?
10. How will achieving these goals impact your life and financial stability?

Setting financial goals, like Alex's journey, is about knowing what you want, understanding what it takes to get there, and aligning your financial habits to reach those milestones. It's a process of constant evaluation and adjustment, but with clear goals in sight, the path becomes much more navigable.

Exercise #2

Practical Exercise:

Create a vision board or goal chart for your financial goals. Include images and numbers that represent what you're working towards. Place it somewhere you can see it daily to keep you motivated and focused.

Chapter 3: Budgeting Basics

Imagine Sarah, a recent college graduate, starting her first full-time job. Excited by her newfound financial independence, she soon finds herself perplexed at how quickly her salary seems to vanish each month. This situation is all too common and underscores the importance of a fundamental financial tool: the budget.

What is a Budget and Why is it Important?

A budget is more than a list of numbers; it's a roadmap for your finances. For Sarah, creating a budget meant she could clearly see the flow of her money—where it comes from and where it goes. Why is this important? Because a budget empowers you to make informed decisions about your spending and saving, ensuring you're not merely drifting along in your financial journey.

Tracking Your Spending Habits

Before Sarah could create a budget, she needed to understand her spending habits. For a month, she tracked every purchase, no matter how small. This exercise can be eye-opening; it's often the little expenses that add up without us realizing it. By tracking her spending, Sarah could identify areas where she could cut back.

Tips for Creating a Realistic Budget

The key to a successful budget is realism. Sarah learned this by initially setting too strict a budget, leading to frustration and inevitable overspending. Your budget should reflect your lifestyle and needs, allowing some flexibility for unforeseen expenses or the occasional treat. It's about balance, not austerity.

Adjusting Your Budget Over Time

A budget is not set in stone. As Sarah's life circumstances changed—like getting a raise or facing unexpected car repairs— she learned to adjust her budget accordingly. Your budget should evolve with your life, always serving as a current guide to your finances.

As you embark on creating your budget, consider these questions and a practical exercise:

1. What are your primary sources of income, and how much do you earn from each?
2. List all your fixed expenses (rent, utilities, and loan payments).
3. What variable expenses do you have (groceries, entertainment, dining out)?
4. How much do you currently save each month?
5. Are there any expenses you can reduce or eliminate?
6. How much would you like to save each month?

7. What financial goals do you need to account for in your budget (like saving for a trip or paying off debt)?
8. How will changes in your income or expenses affect your budget?
9. What system will you use to track your budget (a spreadsheet, an app, or a notebook)?
10. How often will you review and adjust your budget?

Budgeting, as Sarah discovered, is an ongoing process of understanding and adjusting. It's about making your money work for you in the most efficient way possible. With a solid budget in place, you're well on your way to achieving your financial goals.

Exercise #3

Practical Exercise:

For the next month, record every expense and categorize it. At the end of the month, review your spending and identify areas where you can make changes. Use this information to create your first realistic budget.

Chapter 4: Saving Strategies

Meet James, a mid-level manager in his early 40s. Despite a steady job, he often finds himself stressed about financial emergencies and long-term security. His situation highlights a crucial aspect of financial health: saving. This chapter is dedicated to transforming the way we think about and approach saving.

The Importance of Saving

For James, the realization that saving is not just about setting money aside but about building financial security and peace of mind was a game-changer. Saving is essential because it prepares you for unexpected expenses and future plans. It's the buffer that keeps you afloat during tough times and helps you achieve your dreams without undue financial strain.

Different Ways to Save Money

There's no one-size-fits-all approach to saving. James explored various methods, from traditional savings accounts to investing in stocks and bonds. Each method has its advantages and risks, and the key is to find a balance that suits your comfort level and financial goals. Exploring different saving avenues also means you diversify your saving strategies, which can be more effective in the long run.

Setting and Reaching Saving Goals

Setting clear, achievable saving goals was a turning point for James. Whether it's saving for a vacation, a new car, or retirement, having specific targets makes saving more intentional and rewarding. James learned to set both short-term and long-term goals, making saving a regular and purposeful part of his financial plan.

Building an Emergency Fund

One of James's first saving goals was building an emergency fund. This fund is crucial as it provides a financial safety net for unexpected situations, like medical emergencies or sudden job losses. James aimed to save enough to cover at least three to six months of living expenses, giving him peace of mind and financial stability.

As you embark on developing your saving strategies, here are some questions and a practical exercise to guide you:

1. Why is saving money important to you personally?
2. What are your current saving habits?
3. How much money do you want to save in the short term (1 year) and long term (5–10 years)?
4. What specific things are you saving for (e.g., emergency fund, vacation, home renovation)?
5. What different saving methods are you willing to explore

(e.g., high-yield savings accounts, stocks, bonds)?

6. How much of your monthly income can you realistically dedicate to saving?
7. What expenses can you cut back on to increase your savings?
8. How will you track and manage your savings?
9. What challenges do you anticipate in reaching your savings goals?
10. How will achieving your saving goals impact your overall financial health?

For James and for many of us, developing effective saving strategies is a journey of empowerment. It's about taking control of your finances, preparing for the future, and giving yourself the freedom to live your life with financial confidence and security.

Exercise #4

Practical Exercise:

Create a "Savings Plan" for the next year. Include specific goals, the amount you plan to save each month, and the methods you will use. Review and adjust this plan every month based on your progress and any changes in your financial situation.

Chapter 5: Debt Management

Consider the story of Lisa, a 30-year-old marketing consultant who found herself juggling various types of debt. From student loans to credit card bills, her debts were not just financial burdens but also sources of constant stress. Lisa's story is not unique; many people grapple with managing debt. This chapter is about understanding and taking control of your debts, just like Lisa did.

Understanding Different Types of Debt

Lisa's first step was to understand the different types of debt she had. Not all debts are equal; they vary in terms of interest rates, repayment terms, and impact on your financial health. For instance, her student loan had a much lower interest rate compared to her credit card debt. Recognizing these differences helped Lisa prioritize which debts to pay off first.

Strategies for Paying Off Debt

Developing a strategy was Lisa's next challenge. She explored various methods, such as the debt snowball method, where she paid off smaller debts first for psychological wins, and the debt avalanche method, where she tackled debts with the highest interest rates first. Each strategy has its merits, and choosing the right one depends on your financial situation and personal preferences.

How to Avoid High-Interest Debt Traps

One of Lisa's major realizations was the importance of avoiding high-interest debt traps. These are often in the form of credit cards or payday loans, which seem convenient but can quickly spiral out of control due to high interest rates. Lisa learned to be more cautious with her credit card usage and to look for lower interest alternatives whenever possible.

Maintaining a Debt-Free Lifestyle

Finally, Lisa focused on maintaining a debt-free lifestyle. This meant not only paying off her existing debts but also developing habits to prevent falling back into debt. She created a budget to monitor her spending, started building an emergency fund to avoid borrowing for unexpected expenses, and set financial goals to keep her motivated.

As you navigate your own journey of debt management, here are some questions and a practical exercise to help you:

1. List all the debts you currently have, including their interest rates and terms.
2. Which of your debts have the highest interest rates?
3. What are the minimum payments required for each of your debts?
4. Have you considered consolidation or refinancing options

for your debts?

5. What amount can you realistically pay each month towards reducing your debt?
6. Which debt repayment strategy (snowball or avalanche) suits you best?
7. How can you adjust your budget to allocate more funds for debt repayment?
8. What habits or expenses led to your current debt situation?
9. How will being debt-free change your financial situation and lifestyle?
10. What steps can you take to avoid accumulating new debt in the future?

Debt management, as Lisa learned, is not just about clearing balances; it's about gaining financial freedom and peace of mind. With the right strategies and habits, you too can navigate your way out of debt and enjoy the stability and confidence of a debt-free life.

Exercise #5

Practical Exercise:

Create a "Debt Repayment Plan". Outline the order in which you'll tackle your debts, the monthly amount you'll pay, and the target date for becoming debt-free. Review this plan regularly and adjust as needed based on your financial changes.

Chapter 6: Investment Insights

Imagine Kevin, a software engineer in his late twenties. Like many others, Kevin had aspirations of amassing wealth but found the world of investing to be intimidating. His journey from a hesitant beginner to a confident investor mirrors the path many take when stepping into investment waters. This chapter demystifies investing, making it accessible and understandable for everyone, just as it did for Kevin.

Basic Concepts of Investing

Kevin's first lesson was to grasp the basic concepts of investing. He learned that investing isn't just about buying stocks or properties; it's about putting your money into vehicles that have the potential to earn strong rates of return. The goal? To grow your wealth over time. Kevin understood that to be successful, he had to be patient and persistent, as investing is a long-term endeavor.

Understanding Risks and Returns

A crucial aspect of investing that Kevin had to come to terms with was the relationship between risk and return. He learned that generally, the higher the potential returns, the higher the risk. It's essential to assess your risk tolerance—how much risk are you comfortable taking on? Kevin realized that while he was eager to grow his wealth, he wasn't comfortable with high-risk investments, leading him to more conservative investment options.

Different Types of Investments

As Kevin delved deeper, he discovered the plethora of investment options available, from stocks and bonds to mutual funds and real estate, each with its own set of risks and rewards. He learned about diversification—spreading investments across various assets to reduce risk. Kevin started small, choosing investments that aligned with his risk tolerance and long-term financial goals.

Starting Your Investment Journey

The most significant step for Kevin was actually starting his investment journey. He set aside a portion of his income for investments, started reading financial news, and even consulted a financial advisor. He understood that starting small and gradually increasing his investments was a prudent approach.

For those ready to embark on their own investment journey, here are some guiding questions and a practical exercise:

1. What are your primary investment goals (retirement, income generation, and wealth accumulation)?
2. How much do you understand about the stock market, mutual funds, bonds, and real estate investments?
3. What is your risk tolerance? Are you a conservative, moderate, or aggressive investor?
4. How much of your savings can you allocate to investments without impacting your daily financial needs?
5. What investment vehicles align with your financial goals and risk tolerance?
6. How diversified will your investment portfolio be?
7. Are you aware of the fees and taxes associated with different types of investments?
8. How will you stay informed about your investments and the market?
9. What is your long-term plan for your investments?
10. How will you measure the success of your investments?

Investment, as Kevin discovered, is a journey of education, patience, and strategic thinking. It's about making your money work for you, understanding the risks involved, and staying committed to your long-term financial goals. With the right approach, anyone can become a savvy investor.

Exercise #6

Practical Exercise:

Open a mock investment account online to simulate investment strategies without using real money. Track your decisions and progress for a few months to gain understanding and confidence before investing actual funds.

Chapter 7: Retirement Planning

Meet Maria, a dedicated schoolteacher in her mid-forties who suddenly realized that retirement wasn't as far off as it once seemed. Like many, Maria had put off thinking about retirement, assuming it was a concern for the distant future. Her story underscores the importance of early retirement planning, a crucial aspect of long-term financial security.

Why Plan for Retirement early?

Maria learned that the earlier she started planning for retirement, the better. Starting early meant she could take advantage of compound interest, where her savings grow exponentially over time. It also reduced the financial burden she would face if she waited until later in life. For Maria, planning early for retirement transformed it from a source of anxiety into a period of life to look forward to.

Understanding Retirement Accounts

Navigating through different retirement accounts was Maria's next step. She learned about 401(k)s, IRAs, and other retirement savings plans, each with its own set of rules and benefits.

Understanding these options allowed Maria to make informed decisions about where to place her retirement funds for maximum benefit.

Estimating Retirement Needs

Maria also realized the importance of estimating her retirement needs. She considered her desired lifestyle in retirement, potential health care costs, and the impact of inflation. By estimating these costs, Maria could set a realistic savings goal, ensuring she wouldn't outlive her retirement funds.

Strategies for Retirement Savings

Finally, Maria developed a strategy for her retirement savings. This included regularly contributing to her retirement accounts, adjusting her investments based on her age and risk tolerance, and staying informed about changes in retirement laws and policies. She also considered additional saving methods, like investing in real estate or setting up a side business, to supplement her retirement income.

For those beginning their journey of retirement planning, here are some guiding questions and a practical exercise:

1. At what age do you plan to retire, and what kind of lifestyle do you envision?
2. Are you familiar with the different types of retirement accounts available to you (e.g., 401(k), IRA)?
3. How much have you already saved for retirement, and in what types of accounts?
4. What is your current contribution rate to your retirement

savings, and can you increase it?

5. How do you anticipate your expenses will change in retirement?
6. Have you considered the impact of inflation on your retirement savings?
7. What strategies will you employ to maximize your retirement savings?
8. How diversified are your retirement investments?
9. Have you considered potential healthcare costs in your retirement planning?
10. What other income sources can you develop for your retirement years?

Retirement planning, as Maria discovered, is an ongoing process that requires foresight, discipline, and adaptability. It's about envisioning your future, understanding the steps you need to take, and committing to a plan that will secure your financial comfort in your later years. With careful planning, retirement can be a time of relaxation and fulfillment.

Exercise #7

Practical Exercise:

Create a detailed retirement plan. Start by estimating your retirement expenses, then calculate how much you need to save annually to reach your goal, considering your current age and desired retirement age. Review and adjust this plan annually.

Chapter 8: Insurance Understanding

Let's introduce you to Nathan, a 35-year-old entrepreneur who, after a minor car accident, realized the critical importance of having the right insurance. His experience serves as a valuable lesson about understanding and managing insurance needs, a vital aspect of financial planning often overlooked until it's urgently needed.

Types of Insurance You Might Need

Nathan's journey began with recognizing the various types of insurance available. He learned about health insurance, life insurance, auto insurance, and homeowners' or renters' insurance, among others. Each type serves a different purpose, protecting different aspects of your life and assets. Nathan understood that, while not all types of insurance would apply to him, identifying which ones he truly needed was crucial.

Evaluating Your Insurance Needs

The next step for Nathan was to evaluate his insurance needs. This meant considering factors like his lifestyle, dependents, assets, and potential risks. For instance, as a homeowner and a car owner, home and auto insurance were non-negotiable for Nathan. He also thought about his family and opted for life insurance to ensure their financial security in his absence.

Understanding Insurance Policies

Navigating the complexities of insurance policies was a challenge for Nathan. He took the time to understand terms like premiums, deductibles, coverage limits, and exclusions. This knowledge was pivotal in helping him choose policies that offered the best protection for his needs without being over-insured or under-insured.

Balancing Insurance Costs with Benefits

Finally, Nathan learned to balance the costs of insurance with the benefits. He compared different policies, considering both the coverage and the costs. Nathan realized that the cheapest policy isn't always the best option if it doesn't provide adequate coverage. Conversely, the most expensive policy might offer more coverage than he realistically needs.

For those seeking to understand and manage their insurance needs, consider these questions and a practical exercise:

1. What types of insurance are most relevant to your current life situation (health, auto, home, life, etc.)?
2. How does your lifestyle or occupation affect your insurance needs?
3. Do you have dependents who would be financially impacted in the event of your untimely death or disability?
4. What are the values of the assets you need to insure (like

your home or car)?

5. How much can you afford to pay in insurance premiums without straining your budget?

6. Do you understand the terms of your insurance policies, such as coverage limits, deductibles, and exclusions?

7. Have you compared insurance policies from different providers to find the best fit for your needs?

8. How might changes in your life (like buying a house, getting married, or having a child) affect your insurance needs?

9. Are there any discounts or bundled insurance options available that could reduce your costs?

10. How often do you review and update your insurance policies?

Insurance, as Nathan realized, is not just a financial obligation but a crucial element of sound financial planning. It provides peace of mind, knowing that you and your assets are protected against unforeseen circumstances. With the right insurance in place, you can confidently face life's uncertainties.

Exercise #8

Practical Exercise:

Conduct an insurance audit. Review all your current insurance policies to ensure they're up-to-date and meet your current needs. Compare options from different insurers to see if you're getting the best value for your money.

Chapter 9: Tax Knowledge

Meet Emily, a freelance graphic designer who, come tax season, found herself overwhelmed by the complexity of taxes. Her journey from confusion to clarity is a common experience for many, highlighting the necessity of understanding taxes, an essential component of personal finance.

Basics of Taxes

Emily's first step was to grasp the basics of taxes. She learned about different types of taxes, such as income tax, sales tax, and property tax. Understanding how these taxes work, who needs to pay them, and why they are necessary was crucial for her. It allowed Emily to better understand her financial obligations and plan accordingly.

How to Plan for Taxes Efficiently

Planning for taxes efficiently was Emily's next challenge. She realized the importance of setting aside money for taxes throughout the year to avoid the stress of large, unexpected tax bills. Emily also learned about different tax credits and deductions for which she was eligible, significantly reducing her tax liability.

Understanding Tax Benefits

One of the most enlightening aspects for Emily was understanding the various tax benefits available to her, particularly as a freelancer. She explored benefits like home office deductions, health insurance deductions, and retirement savings plans, which all offered tax advantages. These benefits not only reduced her tax burden but also encouraged her to make financially beneficial decisions.

Common Tax Mistakes to Avoid

Finally, Emily focused on learning common tax mistakes to avoid. This included not keeping good financial records, missing deadlines, and not understanding how different income types are taxed. By being aware of these pitfalls, she could ensure she was not paying more taxes than necessary or facing penalties.

For those looking to improve their tax knowledge, here are some questions and a practical exercise:

1. Do you understand the different types of taxes you are required to pay (income, property, sales, etc.)?
2. Are you aware of tax deadlines and the consequences of missing them?
3. Do you know about the tax credits and deductions that you are eligible for?
4. How do you currently track and organize your financial records for tax purposes?
5. If you are self-employed or have a non-traditional income, do you understand how this affects your taxes?
6. Do you know how retirement contributions can affect your

taxable income?

7. Have you ever sought advice from a tax professional, and could this be beneficial for you?

8. Are you aware of common tax-filing mistakes and how to avoid them?

9. How could better tax planning improve your overall financial health?

10. Do you regularly review and update your tax knowledge and strategies?

Emily's journey into the world of taxes taught her that while taxes can be complex, gaining a fundamental understanding is empowering. It allows for smarter financial planning and can significantly impact your overall financial health. With the right knowledge and planning, taxes can be managed effectively and efficiently.

Exercise #9

Practical Exercise:

Create a tax checklist for the upcoming tax season. Include items such as gathering all necessary documents, researching deductions and credits, reviewing last year's return for insights, and setting aside money for any expected tax payments.

Chapter 10: Financial Health Check-ups

Consider the story of Robert, a middle-aged professional who realized the importance of regular financial health check-ups after experiencing sudden market changes and life transitions. His journey underscores the need for continuous monitoring and adaptation of one's financial plan to stay aligned with personal goals and external circumstances.

Regular Review of Your Financial Plan

Robert's first step was to establish a routine for regularly reviewing his financial plan. He set aside time every quarter to assess his budget, savings, investments, and progress towards his financial goals. This regular review helped him stay on track, identify areas needing attention, and celebrate milestones achieved.

Adjusting to Life Changes and Income Fluctuations

Life is dynamic, and so is our financial journey. Robert faced several life changes: a new job, a growing family, and eventually, planning for retirement. Each of these life stages brings different financial needs and priorities. Robert learned to adjust his financial plan in response to these changes, ensuring that his financial strategies remained relevant and effective.

Keeping Up with Economic Changes

Another crucial aspect of Robert's financial health check-ups was staying informed about broader economic changes. Factors like inflation rates, interest rate changes, and stock market fluctuations directly impacted his investments and savings. By keeping an eye on these factors, Robert could make informed decisions to safeguard his financial well-being.

Staying Financially Informed and Educated

Finally, Robert committed himself to ongoing financial education. He regularly read financial news, attended workshops, and sought advice from financial advisors. This continuous learning helped him understand emerging financial trends, new investment opportunities, and potential risks.

For those aiming to maintain robust financial health, consider these questions and a practical exercise:

1. When was the last time you reviewed your financial plan, and how often do you plan to do so?
2. How have recent life changes (like a new job, marriage, or child) impacted your financial goals and plans?
3. Are you aware of how economic changes (like inflation or interest rate fluctuations) can affect your finances?
4. Do you have a strategy for adapting your budget and savings to income fluctuations?
5. How do you track your progress towards long-term finan-

cial goals like retirement?

6. What resources do you use to stay informed about financial news and trends?

7. Have you identified any new financial risks or opportunities that you need to consider in your plan?

8. How do you assess the performance of your investments, and do you know when to make changes?

9. Do you have a network of financial professionals or advisors you can turn to for advice?

10. Are you committed to continually educating yourself about personal finance?

Robert's experience illustrates that financial health is not a static condition but a continuous process. Regular check-ups and adjustments are vital for navigating the ever-changing landscape of personal finance and ensuring long-term stability and peace of mind.

Exercise #10

Practical Exercise:

Conduct a comprehensive annual financial review. Assess all aspects of your financial plan, including income, expenses, savings, investments, insurance, and debt. Adjust your plan based on any changes in your personal life, financial goals, and the economic landscape.

Conclusion

As we draw the curtains on this enlightening journey through "Get Clarity About Your Personal Finance," it's important to pause and reflect on the key takeaways. From understanding your current financial status to the intricacies of investment and the importance of regular financial health check-ups, this book has equipped you with the tools and knowledge to navigate the often complex world of personal finance.

The Journey to Financial Clarity and Freedom

Remember, achieving financial clarity and freedom is a journey, not a destination. The steps outlined in this book are designed to guide you on this path, providing a foundation upon which you can build a secure financial future. Whether you are just starting out or are well into your financial journey, the principles and strategies shared here are timeless and will remain relevant through various stages of your life.

As you close this book, I want to extend a heartfelt thank you for choosing to embark on this journey with me. Your decision to invest in this book is a testament to your commitment to improving your financial well-being, and for that, you should be proud.

A Request for Your Review

Now, I have a small but significant request. If you found value in this book, please consider leaving a review. Your feedback is not only immensely helpful to me but also to others who may be on the fence about embarking on their journey to financial clarity and freedom. Your review can shine a light on the importance of financial literacy and empower others to take that first step towards their own financial health.

Think of your review as a beacon, guiding others who might be lost in the sea of financial uncertainty. Your insights and experiences can resonate with potential readers, helping them understand the significance of the knowledge shared on these pages. By leaving a review, you are contributing to a larger cause: spreading financial awareness and literacy.

Final Words

As you continue on your path to financial independence, remember that the principles and strategies in this book are tools at your disposal. Revisit them often, adapt them to your evolving needs, and never stop learning and growing in your financial journey.

Thank you once again for joining me on this journey. Here's to achieving financial clarity and freedom, one step at a time. Your review can light the way for many others, and together, we can foster a world of financially empowered individuals.

With gratitude,
  Yakalou